BRITISH RAILWAYS

PAST and PRESENT

Nº1 CUMBRIA

by
John Broughton
and
Nigel Harris

Including photographs by
**Derek Cross, Mike Esau, Ron Herbert,
Robert Leslie, Ivo Peters, Peter W. Robinson,
Eric Treacy.**

Silver Link Publishing Ltd

Copyright © Silver Link Publishing, 1985.

First published in the United Kingdom, October 1985

ISBN 0 947971 04 1
Reprinted April 1986
Reprinted October 1988
Reprinted March 1991

Printed and bound in Great Britain by The Amadeus Press Ltd,
Huddersfield, West Yorkshire.

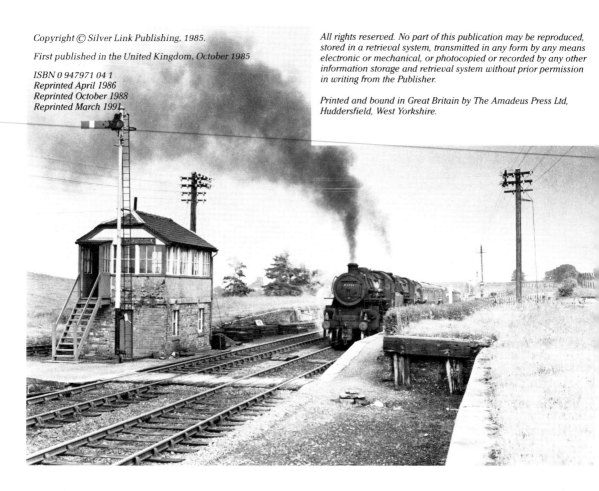

British railways past and present.
Vol. 1 : Cumbria
1. Railroads—Great Britain—History
I. Broughton, John   II. Harris, Nigel
385'.0941   HE3018

ISBN 0-947971-04-1

INTRODUCTION

THE idea for this book first occurred to me during 1980, when as a trainee reporter for 'The Westmorland Gazette' I was charged with the task of compiling the newspaper's regular 'Now and Then' feature, which examined the changing face of Kendal and South Lakeland, using old and new photographs of the same location. It occurred to me then that the once extensive railways of Cumbria would be a good subject for similar treatment and thus 'British Railways Past & Present' was born.

Compiling the book since then with co-author John Broughton has been an enlightening experience. Railway photography is always an enjoyable pastime but countless times in the last few years I have in anger cursed the name of Beeching, and everything he has come to represent. Standing shoulder-high in thick bushes in the old 'NE' yard at Tebay; strolling across the playing fields that now occupy the once-extensive station yard at Silloth-on-Solway; taking a modern photograph on the southern reaches of the Lakeside branch, where even the embankments have been taken away to be used as infill at Greenodd for road improvements on the A590 trunk road. It is difficult to put into words the intensely sad atmosphere of an abandoned railway station or goods yard, but it is a sensation familiar to all

railway enthusiasts who have felt helpless fury at what they see as needless and wasteful railway closures.

Happily the story is not entirely gloomy and this book aims to present a balanced picture of the changing railway activity in Cumbria and some routes have survived to be photographed at work today. The electrified West Coast Main line may have suffered from the photographer's point of view, but at least it is still there and provides a marvellous Anglo-Scottish service in the finest traditions of the LMS, LNWR and Lancaster & Carlisle Companies. The Cumbrian Coast line is still earning its keep and at the time of going to press retained double-track operation and a good deal of semaphore signalling. There are periodic murmurs of track singling and even closure of the Western coastal section but further contraction has not been announced. Most of the stations are now unmanned and served by pay-trains, their goods yards either overgrown or redeveloped. The Coniston branch has been largely reclaimed by nature but happily the northern 3½-mile section of the Lakeside branch continues to run steam trains beyond Haverthwaite, courtesy of the Lakeside & Haverthwaite Railway where I am privileged to be a locomotive driver.

That section of the Settle-Carlisle line lying

FRONT COVER: Ivatt 2-6-0 No. 46441 (now preserved at Steamtown, Carnforth) drifts across the viaduct over the River Crake at Greenodd, on the Lakeside branch with a three-coach local train for Ulverston in 1965, the year in which the passenger service was withdrawn, on September 5. After this date the branch remained open as far as Haverthwaite, for traffic to the iron works at Backbarrow, but the twice weekly goods train was withdrawn and the line closed on April 2 1967, when the ironworks closed its doors. The Haverthwaite-Lakeside section survives under private ownership but at Greenodd the viaduct was demolished to make way for improvements to the A590 road, which was realigned along the trackbed, using spoil from the railway embankment at Haverthwaite village *W. Hubert Foster/JB.*

PREVIOUS PAGE: Shap Wells was always a spectacular location for steam photography and pictured here (top) is Stanier 'Princess Royal' 4-6-2 No. 46209 *Princess Beatrice* storming the grade unassisted with a northbound 12-coach express. The stark beauty of the Westmorland Fells remains unaltered, although the railway has been changed significantly by the electrification to Carlisle and Glasgow in 1974. Also pictured (below) is BR Class 87 Bo-Bo No. 87008 *City of Liverpool*, speeding north with the 9.45 am Euston-Glasgow — 'The Royal Scot' — of March 16 1985. *Eric Treacy (Courtesy P.B. Whitehouse)/JB.*

FACING PAGE: In happier times Penruddock was a typical north country branch line station, located west of Penrith on the beautiful Keswick branch, once part of the grandly named 'Cockermouth, Keswick & Penrith Railway'. Opened by the 'CK&P' in 1864 Penruddock comprised a small station building, goods yard and signal box. The section west of Keswick (to Derwent Junction, Workington) was closed on April 18 1966, the Penrith-Keswick surviving a further six years until March 6 1972 when it too was closed, and Penruddock disappeared from the railway map. The pictures show (top) a special from Euston for the Keswick Convention passing Penruddock box hauled by Ivatt 4MTs Nos. 43121 and 43120 in July 1967, by which time the small loading dock siding had been removed, while the lower picture shows the abandoned remains of the once-picturesque station in March 1985. *Derek Cross/JB.*

BACK COVER: The changing face of Lowgill Junction, on the West Coast Main Line north of Grayrigg. In the top picture, Stanier '5MT' 4-6-0 No. 44832 runs briskly south at the junction at 7 am on September 21 1966 with a lengthy goods train, leaving a perfect trail of exhaust in the still morning air. The Low Gill-Ingleton-Clapham Junction line was already closed at this time, as indicated by the missing signal arm from the bracket signal beyond the signalbox. In the lower picture, 19 years later, class 25s Nos. 25316 and 25324 sprint south past the former junction at 11 am with the Bishopbriggs-Stanlow empty oil tanks (7M50) of April 30 1985. The redundant trackbed remains in use today by BR for access by its S&T engineers road vehicles, for maintenance of lineside electrical equipment. *Ivo Peters/NH.*

within the modern county of Cumbria is featured within these pages and its future — at the time of going to press — was under threat. Loops, sidings, yards and many signalboxes have gone. The line survives as a double track link, apart from the section over Ribblehead Viaduct, supposedly crumbling away, and while the threat of immediate closure seemed to have receeded in 1985 the prospect is still very much part of BR's policy. Leafing through the pages of this book should help ensure that supporters of Britain's railway system remain on their guard, or the 'S&C', and many

other routes, will continue to slip into oblivion, to be reoccupied either by undergrowth and bushes, or the tarmac 'permanent way' of yet another road scheme.

Let us hope that a combination of public support and forward-thinking BR management can produce a rather more optimistic future for our railway network. Let's hope that in the future stations like Appleby will look more like Penrith and less like Penruddock.

NIGEL HARRIS

THE LAST 12 months have been quite an experience for me as I travelled the length and breadth of the county of Cumbria taking some of the 'now' photographs used in this book.

My first impressions were that the railway scene has totally changed over the last 20 to 30 years. Whole areas of the county, especially in the old mining and iron-making areas around Workington and Whitehaven, are now, from a railway point of view, a desert of closed lines, demolished stations and heavily overgrown trackbeds. Only the bridges and the occasional viaduct remain as mute reminders of a more prosperous, bygone age. Another now-closed line which once was one of the most picturesque in the county, is the old Cockermouth, Keswick & Penrith Railway. It was on this line where I came across one of the saddest sights of all. The little station of Penruddock, a few miles west of Penrith, is now a tumbledown ruin. The once attractive station has been allowed to fall down. It is all very depressing.

The railways which are still in operation today have also changed quite dramatically, although there are a few quieter locations which appear not to have changed at all! The West Coast Main Line is now relatively featureless, and most of the old favourite photographic vantage points are now ruined by the catenary system. The Lune Gorge, once one of the most beautiful stretches of the WCML, has been despoiled by the M6 which runs alongside the railway. In fact several photographs taken in this area in the 1960's are just not possible to repeat today. Such is progress. The M6 has also destroyed the site of the junction of the 'CK&P' with the WCML, just south of Penrith. Here a great cutting has been gouged across the landscape involving a new bridge to carry the railway over the motorway.

Tebay, at the north end of the Lune Gorge, was once a bustling railway community with its shed, station and junction. Today at Tebay, you could be forgiven for not knowing that all this once existed. Nothing remains except for a few sidings and a

large overgrown area where the shed once stood. Everywhere, on the railways which are still open, it is very noticeable that the cuttings and embankments are no longer kept tidy as they used to be. Many are now so overgrown as to make photography difficult, if not impossible.

In addition to the physical changes in locations, the traffic on the railways of Cumbria is also very different to what it once was. In the west of the county, the traffic is now reduced to a very few freight trains and a sparse passenger service provided by rather elderly DMUs. A few years ago, the area bustled with mineral workings carrying iron ore, coal and limestone between the mines and quarries and the steel works at Workington. Today only a few chemical, nuclear waste and MGR trains run down the Cumbrian Coast Line. The MGR trains carry coal to Fiddlers Ferry Power Station on Merseyside, and at the time of going to press, even this traffic was reported to be under threat. No longer are there through trains to destinations outside the area from such places as Whitehaven, Workington and Windermere. Today Barrow has only one through train, each way per day, to London.

In common with many main lines, the WCML has lost the vast majority of its stations in the area since there are now only Oxenholme and Penrith stations open between Lancaster and Carlisle. In some cases, all traces of the former stations have disappeared although the station houses still survive in several spots.

JOHN BROUGHTON

OXENHOLME

OXENHOLME station has changed substantially since the days of steam operation: the track layout is considerably simpler but on the other hand the station itself is better equipped, the platforms having been extended northwards in 1975 and southwards in 1880–82. Here we see (above) Oxenholme on July 27 1963 as Stanier 'Jubilee' 4-6-0 No. 45604 *Ceylon* leaves the platform with a Southport-Glasgow train (1S98) while sister '5XP' No. 45697 *Achilles* waits to depart with a Preston-Windermere duty (1L01). On May 12 1984 (left) a class 86 draws into the extended down platform with the 7.26 am Coventry-Glasgow/Edinburgh (1S53) which is stopping to connect with the 10.33 am Oxenholme-Windermere DMU. *Derek Cross/JB*.

INCREDIBLE though it may seem, this is the same location! Above, Stanier '7P' No. 46211 *Queen Maud* sweeps south into Oxenholme with the 'Mid Day Scot' comprised of 13 passenger vehicles and, at the rear of the train, two milk tank wagons. Right: A Glasgow-Euston express speeds south through the station's extended platforms behind a class 86 on May 12 1984. The station dates from 1846 when it was built by the Lancaster & Carlisle and Kendal & Windermere Railway Companies, and the changing fortunes of the Windermere branch are clearly apparent. The double-turnout junction was taken out of use from May 13 1968 and today the once double-track busy branch is reduced to 'long siding' status from Oxenholme and is capable of DMU operation only, there being no run-round loop at Windermere. The extension of the platforms across the site of the junction put an end to the long-standing tradition of expresses having to draw up twice. *Alec Mayor/JB*.

THE WINDERMERE BRANCH

TRAINS leaving Oxenholme for Windermere ran for two miles on a 1 in 80 falling gradient before reaching Kendal station, which opened its doors for business when the Kendal & Windermere Railway formally opened on April 20 1847. The station (behind the photographer) had up and down platforms and an impressive building, sadly derelict and threatened with demolition as this book went to press. These views show the changes in the goods yard area, on the Windermere side of the station. The goods yard, visible to the left of No. 45586 *Mysore* as it charges the climb to Oxenholme with a train of MK.1 stock, had 14 principal roads and a substantial traffic in general merchandise, but principally coal — six merchants were supplied by the railway. A huge goods shed, now converted for business use, had two roads and the yard was very busy until the 1960s: rundown was rapid and closure took place on May 1 1972. The goods yard today has been redeveloped for light industrial use and the once busy branch now sees only its DMU shuttle. *Alec Mayor/NH.*

SUBSTANTIAL change has also taken place here, about ½-mile east of the village of Staveley, where the Windermere branch crosses the A591. In the upper picture, 'Patriot' 4-6-0 No. 45537 *Private E. Sykes VC* approaches the gated and manned crossing with a Windermere-London train on March 31 1949. The heavy traditional white wooden gates were replaced by automatic half-barriers on October 16 1967, and the branch was singled from April 30 1973. The former crossing-keeper's cottage survives as a private dwelling. The lower picture shows the 9.16 am Oxenholme-Windermere DMU passing the crossing on March 23 1985. *John Porter/JB.*

WINDERMERE station is a sorry sight today, a much reduced shadow of a once-bustling terminus which brought large quantities of freight and thousands of passengers into the Lakes every year. The single shortened platform (the train shed has been abandoned by BR and converted into a supermarket even since this picture was taken in 1984) is the end of a 'long siding' from Oxenholme. The lack of a run-round loop prevents the operation of locomotive-hauled specials to Windermere and this has been a point of much criticism in recent years. The Lakeland terminus, whose opening in 1847 had been bitterly opposed by the poet Wordsworth, once boasted four platforms, a signal box, engine shed, turntable, carriage sidings, goods shed and coal yard. In happier times more than 60 railwaymen worked here but traffic ebbed away seriously after 1960 and the familiar pattern of contraction, cutback and tracklifting was set in motion. The goods yard closed in 1969 even though the daily goods brought in large quantities of coal and Windermere's merchants had to travel to Kendal for their supplies. Their frustration must have been compounded by the fact that the disused sidings at Windermere were not lifted until 1972! *Alec Mayor/NH.*

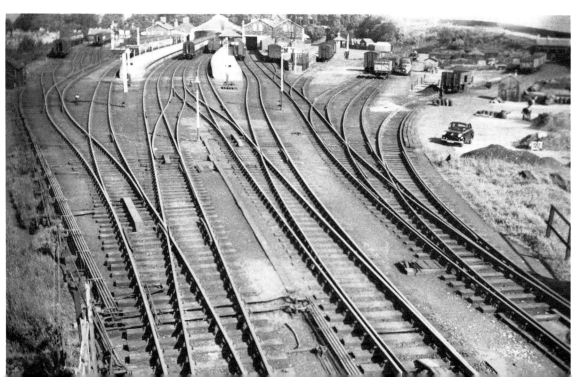

WITH the end of steam operation on BR metals just a few hours away, Stanier 5MT 4-6-0 No. 44894 shunts the Windermere-Carnforth goods, at Windermere, on August 1 1968. At busy periods these sidings would be used for the stabling of passenger stock, but the station's substantial goods traffic included timber, coal, coke, cattle, animal feed, flour, cars gunpowder (from Elterwater) and fish, and daily traffic usually involved 50 or more wagons. The land was sold following closure of the goods yard in 1969, after which Lakeland Plastics established its thriving factory on the site. *Derek Cross/JB.*

LEFT: Windermere station, post-1985. After 134 years of service as the area's principal railhead British Rail announced in 1981 that plans were afoot to sell the train shed and station buildings at Windermere to E.H. Booth & Co. Ltd., for conversion into a supermarket. BR said that it could not afford to repair the station buildings and that demolition might be the only alternative to this plan. After much local discussion the scheme was approved and the supermarket was opened in 1985. This is the view today from what was the platform end, adjacent to the bufferstops. *JB*.

IN June 1967 this was the view from the same spot as English Electric Type 4 (later class 40) No. D 387 stands at the bufferstop with a Preston-Windermere passenger train. Windermere used to have direct passenger links with the Midlands, Bradford, Leeds, Liverpool Lime Street, Birmingham, Preston, Blackpool, Manchester and Morecambe in addition to four daily links with London (including 'The Lakes Express') and 14 local trains to Oxenholme. In the inter-war years 17 specials could converge on Windermere on a summer Sunday: by 1972 a total of just 14 summer specials ran to Windermere. The London trains had gone by 1970 and today there is normally just the DMU to Oxenholme, though in 1985 a Sunday through service ran from Manchester Victoria. *Derek Cross*.

GRAYRIGG

Facing page & left: The West Coast Main Line has seen many changes in the 17 years which separate these two studies of Grayrigg but apart from the loss of the down sidings and the realignment of the main lines for higher speed running, the track layout remains basically unchanged. On the facing page English Electric Type 4 diesel-electric No. D 221 heads south on August 5 1967 with the 11.22 am Perth Birmingham (1M37) while a Stanier 5MT 4-6-0 waits for the road in the up loop. By this time the station (which closed on February 1 1954) had already been swept away: the signalbox, opened in 1926 when it replaced an earlier LNWR type, closed in April 1973 when power signalling took over. In the modern picture (left) the 9.31 am Carlisle-Preston passes Grayrigg in the charge of an unidentified class 81. The loops, which survive today, were first installed in 1925/6 and were modified further in the late 1960s: they are used to hold freight trains while more important passenger services speed past, a function for which they were first installed, in conjunction with accelerations in the timetable for the introduction of the 'Royal Scot' by the LMS in 1927. Langdale Fell still broods over the scene in the background.
Facing page: John Clarke/Greater Manchester Museum of Science & Industry; Left: JB.

Low Gill

Right: After closure of the Low Gill - Ingleton - Clapham Junction line in March 1965 it was used for the dumping of spent ballast and occasional diversions. On July 29 1965 Ivatt 4MT 2-6-0 No. 43017 had been to Sedbergh to collect some empty wagons, and is seen here hauling its train over the elegant Beck Foot viaduct, approaching Low Gill Junction.
Ivo Peters.

Left: Beck Foot Viaduct still stands today, and a commanding view of the structure can be had from the M6, which now runs behind the photographer. Opened in 1861, this line was closed to passenger traffic on February 1 1954, but it remained open for goods traffic until March 1 1965, when the line's last goods depot, at Ingleton, closed. The track was lifted in 1967. *NH.*

SEDBERGH

OPENED to freight traffic on August 24 1861 and passengers on September 16 1861, the Clapham-Ingleton-Low Gill line ran through picturesque countryside, and gave the Midland Railway a route to Scotland, (via the L&CR) a role later taken over in 1876 by its spectacularly engineered Settle-Carlisle line across the Fells. Above: an Ivatt Class 4MT 2-6-0 shunts a mixture of BR standard 16-ton steel mineral wagons and single-vent box vans at Sedbergh station goods yard, which closed on October 1 1964. Right: Sedbergh yard still handled coal traffic when this picture was taken in September 1984, but transported entirely by lorry on the region's twisting roads. *Derek Cross/JB.*

THE Low Gill-Clapham Junction line closed to regular passenger traffic on February 1 1954, after stations at Ingleton, Kirkby Lonsdale, Barbon and Sedbergh all issued tickets for the last time. However Sedbergh station remained in periodic use until 1964 for use by specials carrying pupils to the town's famous school. Top: Coupled to the self-weighing tender used in assessments of a locomotive's coal consumption, Stanier 'Black 5' 4-6-0 No. 45081 stands at Sedbergh in brilliant sunshine with 1T41, the last Sedbergh school special, from Carlisle, on September 17 1964. The line's last goods depot, at Ingleton, closed its doors on March 1 1965, ending all regular traffic between Low Gill and Clapham, however the link was subsequently used for occasional diversions, the storage of surplus wagons and the dumping of spent ballast before it was finally lifted, demolition operations starting in April 1967. Above: A latterday view from the same position, all evidence of the trackbed and platforms obliterated by a putting green. *Derek Cross/IB.*

THE LUNE GORGE

THIS is one of the most picturesque settings through which the West Coast Main line runs: the steep fellsides tower above the track on both sides whilst the railway skirts the western slopes, towards Tebay.

Above: snowplough-fitted Stanier 5MT No. 45295 drifts south with an up train of mixed empty ballast hoppers on April 17 1967. This pleasant scene was rudely shattered when the M6 carved its way noisily through the gorge, following the railway as far as Tebay, where the road and railway diverge for the climb over Shap Fell. In the modern scene (right) an unidentified class 87 speeds south with an up express alongside the motorway. *Ivo Peters/NH.*

TEBAY

TEBAY once featured a busy station, locomotive shed and junction with the NE 'Stainmore' line: today there are just three sidings on the down side of the main line. Above: 'EE' type 4 No. D 299 forges past Tebay No. 1 signalbox with the down 'Royal Scot' while 6P 'Royal Scot' 4-6-0 No. 46140 *The King's Royal Rifle Corps* waits in the loop with a permanent way special, on July 16 1965. Left: the same spot today, devoid of signals and much reduced in character. Class 86s Nos. 86 325 and 86 320 speed north with a heavy freight on June 29 1984. *Derek Cross/JB*.

THE important junction station at Tebay has been completely erased from the landscape and the NER link to Darlington is now but a memory. In the top picture, taken from Tebay No. 2 signal box, a Manchester-Glasgow train is hurried towards Shap by 'Riddles' Britannia 'Pacific' No. 70052 *Firth of Tay*, piloted by Fowler 2-6-4T No. 42322. Tebay station closed on July 1 1968 and remained derelict for three years before being demolished and the site levelled. The engine shed was closed on January 1 1968 and demolished. Three sidings and a down loop (converted from a refuge siding in 1925) survive. In the modern scene (right) class No. 86 018 begins Shap's four mile climb at Tebay with a northbound parcels on Tuesday April 30 1985. *Derek Cross/NH.*

EAST FROM TEBAY

TEBAY was the point at which North Eastern Railway metals from Darlington joined the West Coast Main Line, and the importance of this further stimulated the development of Tebay as a railway settlement. Originally known as the South Durham & Lancashire Union Railway, this link was designed to provide a through route between the ports of Eastern and Western England, though in practice the line was used primarily to link the respective regions iron and steel works. Top: Stanier 5MT 4-6-0 No. 45096 drifts past Tebay Yard No. 3 signalbox, on the final approach from the NE to Tebay station and the junction with the WCML, with a Newcastle-Blackpool train in August 1960. Above: the same location in June 1984, 19 years after closure of the yard and 22 years after closure of the NE route from Tebay, via Barnard Castle. A small pile of rubble marks the spot of the small signalbox: behind the photographer part of the yard has been developed as a small industrial area named 'The Sidings' as a reminder of its previous role. The trackbed here is used today as a footpath and unofficial cycletrack. *Derek Cross/JB.*

THE NER formation from Tebay was used at its western end after closure in 1962 to reconstruct the A685 road, which follows the railway route from Tebay to Ravenstonedale. This gives the road a very level aspect, with sweeping curves and it is likely that very few of the motorists speeding over the tarmac know its former role. Probably even fewer care. In the top picture, Riddles 4MT 2-6-0 No. 76049 and Ivatt 4MT No. 43036 roll the last mile or so into Tebay on July 22, 1961 with a Darlington-Blackpool train. Below: the same scene in June 1984 — the gently undulating hills remain unchanged, but the railway is long gone. *Derek Cross/JB.*

Gaisgill station, pictured (top) in the early years of this century, was the first station from Tebay on the NER route. The locomotive is NER 2-4-0 No. 167, one of Edward Fletcher's last express classes built in two varieties: the 901 class (with 7 ft diameter driving wheels) and the 1440 class (with 6 ft wheels). No. 167 (a 901 class) was one of a batch of these engines regularly used on the Stainmore line: a total of 55 of the 901 type were built between 1872 and 1882. This picture shows No. 167 following the fitting of a larger boiler and cab in 1906, and it is in splendid condition. The station was closed to passengers on December 1 1952, the route itself was closed in 1962 and the Tebay-Ravenstonedale section subsequently used as the basis for the A685 road. The later picture shows Gaisgill on Tuesday April 30 1985. *J.W. Pinch Collection/NH.*

THE attractive country station at Ravenstonedale (pictured top on January 28 1962) was located on the NER Durham-Barnard Castle-Tebay line, which once carried a very brisk two-way traffic in coke and iron ore between the industrial areas of South Durham and the Furness area. The station lost its passenger traffic on December 1 1952 although seasonal passenger workings continued until September 2 1961. The last passenger train (an enthusiasts special) ran on January 20 1962, after which the Barnard Castle-Tebay link was closed. Ravenstonedale station — which was actually nearer Newbiggin — is now a private residence. The trackbed here has vanished beneath a paddock whilst the overbridge has been filled in — although its parapet is still smoke blackened as a reminder of its past. *Ron Herbert/NH.*

KIRKBY STEPHEN East was the location where the Tebay-Durham link was joined by the NER route from Eden Valley Junction, near Penrith, on the West Coast Main line. The station was thus larger than might have been expected at a small town: the extensive sidings were needed to handle the substantial mineral traffic. There was also an engine shed. Closed on January 20 1962, the station buildings survive in industrial use. On the other side of the A685 road — which is carried over the railway site on an impressive viaduct best viewed from the abandoned trackbed — the goods yard is occupied by the local coal merchant. The station is pictured (above) on January 28 1962 and (left) in May 1985. *Ron Herbert/JB.*

THE imposing Belah Viaduct, between Barras and Kirkby Stephen, towered 196 ft above the River Belah in wild, bleak moorland. Its total length was 1,040 ft and a signal box (whose derelict remains are visible in the September 1984 picture) was sited at the western end. Running through very difficult country, the 35 miles between Barnard Castle and Tebay took four years to complete: it was often said that this railway experienced nine months winter and three months bad weather! Dismantled shortly after the link closed in 1962, only the viaduct abutments and crumbling piers in the valley bottom remain as mute reminders of one of Britain's wildest railways. Top: Riddles '2MT' 2-6-0 No. 78016 and '4MT' 2-6-0 No. 76024 rumble cautiously across the girders with the 11.20 am Blackpool-Newcastle of July 18 1959. *Robert Leslie/JB*.

SHAP

THE little signal box at Scout Green served two purposes. It was an intermediate box between Tebay and Shap and it also controlled a level crossing on the minor road linking Scout Green village with the B626 Orton-Shap road. Above: a Stanier 'Black 5' 4-6-0 thunders unaided past Scout Green with a down parcels train before breakfast on April 22 1965. The colour light signal on the up road was installed on June 9 1963, replacing a very tall LNWR semaphore signal. The level crossing closed when the M6 was built and the signalbox was demolished following commissioning of the power signalling system in 1973. Left: on August 22 1985 a class 86 climbs effortlessly past Scout Green with a down parcels train as a class 87 hurries downgrade with a southbound passenger.
Ivo Peters/NH.

THE four gruelling miles of 1 in 75 from Tebay to Shap Summit was a real test of the steam engineman's mettle, especially in the harsh weather which frequently lashed the Westmorland fells. In fine weather this notorious incline was a popular attraction for many photographers, especially the late and sadly missed Derek Cross and Eric Treacy: both men inspired a generation of railway enthusiasts to pick up their cameras. Top: In beautiful sunny weather, 'Royal Scot' 4-6-0 No. 46135 *The East Lancashire Regiment* forges steadily towards Shap Summit, about ½-mile distant, with a rake of LMS stock forming a Birmingham-Glasgow train. Above: On June 23 1984 a class 86 follows the same path at Shap Wells with a northbound parcels train. In the distance the peace of the fells is disturbed by traffic on the M6 whilst on the railway, where the overhead power supply has replaced the lineside pole route, electric locomotives speed effortlessly north, apparently oblivious of the gradient which 20 years ago caused steam traction to put on a spectacular show. *Eric Treacy/JB.*

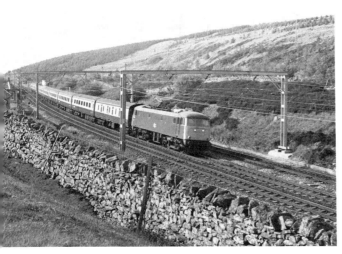

SHAP SUMMIT was the high-point of the LNWR route from the English lowlands to the Scottish border at Carlisle. It was the location where, in the days of steam, the crews of northbound trains could look forward to a downhill run after the taxing climb from sea-level just north of Lancaster. The distinctive Summit signalbox, visible in the background of the 1964 picture, was a busy place: many northbound trains were assisted to the Summit and the 'bankers' had to run back to Tebay between the procession of southbound trains. Banking ceased with the advent of more modern traction, and with the coming of power signalling in 1973 the box was closed and demolished. The summit cutting, ¼-mile long and 60 ft deep, was excavated by 500 men who used 23 tons of gunpowder to blast out the Westmorland rock! Top: Rebuilt 'Patriot' 4-6-0 No. 45522 *Prestatyn* begins the descent to Tebay with an Edinburgh-Birmingham duty in July 1964. Note the LNWR lower quadrant starting signal in the up loop. Above left: 20 years later at the same spot. Heading south on June 16 1984 is a class 86 locomotive with the 3.20 pm Glasgow-Euston express. *Derek Cross/JB*. Above right: A view of the maroon enamel summit board, August 17 1954. *BR*

FORMERLY known as Clifton North Junction, Eden Valley Junction (3¼ miles south of Penrith) marked the convergence of the WCML and the NER's cross-country 'Stainmore' line. Opened on August 1 1863, this junction superseded the former south-facing connection with the WCML at Clifton, this spur being lifted in 1875. On July 12 1963 (top) Ivatt 2MT 2-6-0 No. 46455 ambles across the junction onto the down main line with a single hopper wagon and brakevan forming the Clifton Moor shunt. Note the three varieties of signals in use: LMS upper quadrant and NER and LNWR lower quadrant types. The LNWR signalbox was opened on June 19 1905 and closed on March 19 1973, when power signalling took over. Right: apart from the isolated buffer-stop, there is little evidence today that this once-neat junction ever existed. Class 31 No. 31 428 rumbles past on March 9 1985: the days of neatly manicured ballast are clearly long gone. *Derek Cross/JB.*

KESWICK JUNCTION, controlled by Penrith No. 1 signalbox, was the point where the Cockermouth Keswick & Penrith line met the WCML, one mile south of Penrith station. This cross-Lakeland link was opened to mineral traffic on October 26 1864, and passenger trains on January 2 1865. Stanier 'Jubilee' 4-6-0 No. 45737 *Atlas* approaches the junction (the 'CK&P' is on the right) on August 18 1962 with a down express comprised entirely of LMS stock. The location is scarcely recognisable today, as the M6 motorway now carves its way through the landscape, the WCML being carried over the road by a concrete viaduct featuring two 100 ft spans and one 158 ft span. This bridge was built in 1967–8, the Penrith by-pass section of the M6 opening in 1968. On June 29 1984 No. 87 025 *County of Cheshire* crosses the M6 with a down passenger duty: part of the 'CK&P' alignment here is occupied today by the down goods loop. *Derek Cross/JB*. Above left: Entry to Penrith from the 'CK&P' was controlled by these bracketed LNWR lower quadrant semaphores, pictured on August 15 1959. *Robert Leslie*

THE COCKERMOUTH, KESWICK & PENRITH RAILWAY

TRAINS leaving the WCML at Penrith bound for West Cumbria over the 'CK&P' metals faced a stiff task from the outset — its first four miles climbed at 1 in 70 through the attractive little station at Penruddock (see page 2) to the summit, 889 ft above sea level, just east of Troutbeck. This pleasant hamlet is located in a delightful valley and the station once boasted a goods yard and signalbox. Built in 1864, the station survived until March 1972, when the truncated 'long siding' from Penrith to Keswick was closed and lifted. Goods carried on this railway once included lead mined near Troutbeck. In the final days of operation (right), a two-car DMU (displaying 'Accrington' on its destination blind!) starts from Troutbeck on February 19 1972, bound for Keswick on the 1 in 62½ falling gradient to Threlkeld. On this section the line descended nearly 400 ft in four miles. This picture was taken from a road overbridge which was demolished in 1984 — a level crossing would be needed today. The station building is now in private ownership, a neat lawn extending across the trackbed, while the signalbox stands in derelict isolation (top right), the platform edging stones dumped on the former trackbed. The later pictures were taken on August 22 1985.
Peter W. Robinson/NH.

THE 'CK&P', though now largely forgotten, was one of this country's most beautiful and scenic railways. In this marvellous scene (top) LNWR 'Cauliflower' 2F 0-6-0 No. 58409 approaches Troutbeck from Threlkeld with a rake of 15 assorted mineral wagons, including a pair of steel-bodied BR 16-ton standard vehicles. Allocated to Penrith shed (12C), the vintage engine has been fitted with an apparently home-made wooden shelter on the front of the tender. In today's scene, the realigned A66 carries a noisy procession of cars and lorries past the abandoned trackbed, now used only by the local farmers. In the background the distinctive saddleback mountain Blencathra surveys the scene as it always did. *Eric Treacy (Courtesy P.B. Whitehouse/NH.*

THRELKELD, between Troutbeck and Keswick presents a very sorry sight today: the trackbed is overgrown and the island platform's attractive station building — which featured an integral signalbox — was in ruins when the later picture (centre right) was taken in March 1985. On May 8 1963 (above) the 9.45 am Workington-Carlisle DMU is starting the climb to Troutbeck at Threlkeld, which marked the start of the 13½-mile double track section to Penruddock. This doubling had been authorised in June 1894 as a consequence of heavy seasonal passenger traffic. DMUs took over the line's passenger service from January 3 1955, when it was judged that the link had a rosy future: by 1960 annual losses were in the region of £50,000, and an altogether gloomier future loomed with final closure of this section taking place in 1972. Below right: The crumbling remains of the distinctive station building and signal box in 1984. *Ron Herbert/JB/NH.*

KESWICK, centrally placed between Penrith and Workington in the heart of the Lake District, was an important railhead, primarily for tourist traffic, and a large hotel was built adjacent to the railway, linked to the station by a covered walkway from the down platform. In addition to regular passenger and freight workings there was an annual surge in traffic each July when an evangelical convention held in the town generated a number of special trains which were usually double headed by Ivatt 2MT 2-6-0s. Declining traffic led to the withdrawal of through goods workings from June 1 1964 and the line west of Keswick was closed from April 18 1966. Objections in Keswick saved the link to Penrith however and this survived as a 'long siding', with all stations operating as unstaffed halts, from July 1 1968 to March 6 1972 when the last DMU shuttle ran. The station at Keswick fell into decay and the up island platform and buildings were subsequently flattened, leaving the main building to gradually decay further. Part of it has been used as a small museum by the Derwent Railway Society. Top: Ivatt class 2MT 2-6-0s Nos. 46458 and 46426 arrive at Keswick with the SLS Lakes & Fells excursion of April 2 1966, comprised of LMS stock. Above: the same viewpoint on March 2 1985. *Derek Cross/JB.*

THIS section of the 'CK&P', near Bassenthwaite Lake, is another piece of railway which has suffered the ignominy of having had a road superimposed onto its route; in this instance it is the A66 Penrith-Workington road. *Below:* running over the neatly-manicured permanent way on May 7 1963 is a two-car DMU forming the 5.00 pm Penrith-Workington service. This section of route west of Keswick, erased from the railway map overnight on April 18 1966, remained derelict and overgrown until the road builders came and today's drivers enjoy a fast road, with sweeping curves. Many people seriously question the logic of turning railways like this into roads which now carry a constant stream of large, heavy lorries through the heart of the National Park but the strength of the pro-roads lobby will doubtless prompt further examples of this action. *Ron Herbert/JB.*

BASSENTHWAITE LAKE station, once an attractive country station set amongst the Lakeland hills, on the shores of Bassenthwaite Lake, had all but disappeared when the later picture was taken in April 1985. The station house survives but the platforms are long gone and nature has taken over where the trains once ran. Travellers on the neighbouring A66 rarely realise that the little station ever existed: the A66 runs on the trackbed on both sides of the station. Above: in happier times, Ivatt 2MT 2-6-0 No. 46491 drifts off the single track and onto the station's passing loop with a short mixed goods on May 7 1963. *Ron Herbert/JB.*

Above: On April 17 1949 LNWR 'Cauliflower' 0-6-0 No. 28588 (LMS number) coasts over the River Cocker bridge at the eastern end of Cockermouth station with a Penrith-Workington service of four coaches. The signalman is ready to collect the single line tablet for the previous section and in exchange give the driver the tablet giving him authority to proceed onto the next single line section, to Cockermouth Junction. The concrete bridge on March 2 1985 (below) was abandoned, stripped of ballast and covered in graffiti. Bridges were a prominent feature of the 'CK&P' which featured staggering 135 such structures along its 31¼-mile length. *John Porter/JB*.

COCKERMOUTH was the first town on the 'CK&P' route to enjoy the benefits of a railway link when the Cockermouth & Workington Railway opened on April 28 1847, giving the Cumberland town of around 5,000 people access to the West Coast via an 8¼-mile branch line to Derwent Junction. When the 'CK&P' came in 1864 it proved impossible to use the existing C&WR terminus and when the through route was constructed the old station, at the end of a ½-mile branch, was redesignated as the town's goods depot. The station illustrated (top) was therefore provided on the south side of the town, where on April 17 1949 LNWR 'Cauliflower' 0-6-0 No. 28580 (LMS number) waits with a Workington-Penrith train. Note the marvellous gas lamp standards and the little boy being instructed about the engine! This station site remained derelict for many years following closure in 1966 and demolition of the buildings. However, in 1985 Cumbria Fire Service moved in and by March of that year a large new headquarters building was well under way (above). *John Porter/JB.*

PENRITH

PENRITH developed as a major junction station as a consequence of the opening of the Eden Valley and 'CK&P' routes and activity in the station and yards was once intense, with passenger services on the WCML connecting with cross-country services to both West Cumberland and the NE. Above: On July 16 1965 Ivatt 2MT 2-6-0 No. 46513 shunts in Penrith yard whilst Stanier 5MT 4-6-0 No. 45369 steams past on the main line with the Carlisle-Hardendale (Shap Quarry) empties. Right: Class 86 No. 86 311 *Airey Neave* passes the abandoned yard site with an up passenger working, June 29 1984. The LNWR locomotive shed in the background of the 1965 picture was closed in 1962 and has since been demolished: only a few stone blocks mark its passing. The goods yard closed from January 7 1971 although a small rail-served coal concentration depot remained, but this too disappeared before electric services commenced in May 1974. *Derek Cross/JB*.

APART from Oxenholme, Penrith is the only other WCML station to survive between Lancaster and Carlisle: stations which disappeared into the history books on L&CR metals are (together with closure dates): Hest Bank (February 3 1969); Bolton le Sands (February 3 1969); Carnforth (WCML platforms only — May 4 1970); Burton & Holme (March 27 1950); Milnthorpe (July 1 1968); Grayrigg (February 1 1954); Low Gill (March 7 1960); Tebay (July 1 1968); Shap (July 1 1968); Clifton & Lowther (July 4 1938); Plumpton (May 31 1948); Calthwaite (April 7 1952); Southwaite (April 7 1952); Wreay (August 16 1943); Brisco (closure date uncertain — but probably circa 1852). Above: On June 13 1964 Ivatt 2MT 2-6-0s Nos. 46246 and 46458 pass Penrith No. 1 signalbox with an RCTS special from Leeds, bound for the 'CK&P' route. Below: The same spot on August 22 1985 as 85 016 speeds south with the 8.35 am Mossend-Severn Tunnel Junction Railfreight working (6V93). *Derek Cross/NH.*

CARLISLE

A RAILWAY centre of great significance, Carlisle once hosted the operations of seven companies in the pre-Grouping years: the LNWR, CR, NER, MCR, NBR, MR and GSWR. Much tension and dispute accompanied the steady development of these different companies, which all had engine sheds and goods depots in the 'Border City'. For the railway enthusiast it presented an unparalleled spectacle of variety and colour and many working practices remained unchanged until the 1960s. Above: Stanier 'Jubilee' 4-6-0 No. 45564 *New South Wales* heads the up 'Waverley' during rebuilding of the station roof in 1957/8. Right: nearly 30 years later, class 87 No. 87 017 *Iron Duke* waits under the wires with the up 'Clansman' of July 21 1984. *Eric Treacy/JB.*

ONE OF the Companies operating into Citadel station prior to 1923 was the Maryport & Carlisle Railway, whose trains used platform 2 — or the 'M&C bay' as it was known. Above: On April 26 1985 the 1 pm Whitehaven-Carlisle DMU maintains this platform's link with the Cumbrian coast line. Below: Class 2P 4-4-0 No. 40396 stands in the same location with an arrival from Whitehaven on August 7 1954. The superb Gothic end-screens of the massive overall roof disappeared during the rebuilding of 1957/8. In addition to the WCML and the West Cumbrian Coast, Carlisle today is the hub of other routes to Leeds, Stranraer and Newcastle. *Robert Leslie/JB.*

PASSENGER services from Carlisle in years past featured trains to Edinburgh over the rugged 'Waverley route', via Riccarton Junction. This main line closed on January 6 1969 and has since been lifted, but it still holds a special place in the affections of many railway enthusiasts. Above: On April 22 1962 LNER A1 'Pacific' No. 60132 *Marmion*, carrying a 52A (Gateshead) shedplate, leaves the 'NB bay' at the north end of Carlisle station with the 1.22 pm Carlisle-Edinburgh Waverley. Right: the same scene almost exactly 23 years later as class 87 No. 87 013 *John O'Gaunt* sets back into the station with a pair of parcels vans, April 26 1985.
Ron Herbert/JB.

ANOTHER extinct passenger link from Carlisle was the service to Langholm, the terminus of a branch which diverged from the 'Waverley route' at Riddings Junction. Above: Ivatt 4MT 2-6-0 No. 43139 coasts into Carlisle station, past No. signalbox, with a two-coach working from Langholm on April 22 1962. Note the tablet-catcher on the tender-side. The Riddings-Langholm branch closed on June 15 1964, five years before the 'Waverley route' itself passed into the history books. Below: Electrification and power signalling has transformed this location, the LNWR box and semaphore signals giving way to colour lights and a complex web of catenary masts and wires. Class 86 228 *Vulcan Heritage* glides into Carlisle on April 26 1985 with an up express. *Ron Herbert/JB*.

CARLISLE KINGMOOR

KINGMOOR SHED, (12A in later BR classification) was sited 1¾-miles north of Carlisle Citadel station and was built in the late 1870s. The shed and yard are visible behind Stanier 'Black 5' 4-6-0 No. 45174 (left) heading north with an 18-vehicle van train, in the mid 1960s. In the 1950s Carlisle's goods traffic included the weekly handling of up to 30,000 wagons, many of which would be 'tripped' perhaps twice between yards by up to 18 locomotives engaged on inter-yard duties, and this led to the major proposals in the Modernisation Plan of 1955 for a new hump yard at Carlisle. Work on the £4½ million yard, on a 2½-mile × ¼-mile strip of land on the western side of the WCML behind the photographer, started in 1959 and the tracks converging from the right were laid to give direct access to the yard from the city's goods lines. The yard was of course never fully utilised and this link, opened in 1963, was closed within six years. Top: Riddles 5MT 4-6-0 No. 73062 passes Kingmoor, before the goods line yard link was laid, on March 28 1959 with a down freight from Dentonholme yard. Above: Kingmoor on August 13 1984 as a lone class 08 shunter ambles south toward Citadel; a sad contrast to the busy scenes of the 50s and 60s.
Opposite: Eric Treacy (Courtesy P.B. Whitehouse);
Top: Robert Leslie; Above: JB.

Above: the impressive scene at the south end of Kingmoor shed on May 3 1959 as Stanier 5MT No. 44903 passes Etterby Junction with the Broughton (near Symington)-London meat train. Kingmoor shed, on the right, closed in December 1967 in the last months of steam traction on the national network to be replaced by Kingmoor Traction Maintenance Depot, which opened in January 1968 on the opposite side of the WCML. Right: the view from the same location today is far less impressive for the railway photographer or train-spotter. The shed site is now overgrown and abandoned, the signalbox and manual signalling is long gone and the sidings on the left were used only for the stabling of condemned stock when the later picture was taken on April 26 1985. No. 87 014 *Knight of the Thistle* is heading south with a passenger service comprised of Mk 1 and Mk 3 stock. *Robert Leslie/JB.*

Left: This spot, just a few miles north of Carlisle and just south of the Scottish border, at Rockcliffe, has seen many changes in the 26 years separating these two photographs. On August 1 1958 a gang of three platelayers work on changing sleepers undisturbed by the passing on the up line of Stanier 'Jubilee' 4-6-0 No. 45724 *Warspite* and Riddles 7MT 4-6-2 No. 70054 *Dornoch Firth* with a Glasgow-Manchester express, comprised of a mixture of Mk. 1 and pre-Nationalisation LMS passenger stock. The 'Jubilee' is coupled to a narrow Fowler tender. *Robert Leslie.*

Right: The same location on August 13 1984 with a class 86 in attendance at the head of the 9.50 am Glasgow-Poole (1025). The up and down goods lines have disappeared and in the distance can be seen the concrete flyover built to give up trains direct access to Carlisle new yard, which was completed during 1963. In 1965 the yard, situated south-west of the photographer, was handling 4,250 wagons a day, but the changeover from wagon-load to block train working eroded usefulness of the yard, which never realised its full potential. The down section of the yard was progressively closed in 1972 and ten years later hump-shunting gave way to manual operation, thus defeating the object of building the automated yard in the first place! The up yard was still operational — although only just — in 1985. *Robert Leslie/JB.*

THE 'LONG DRAG'

THE small village of Cumwhinton, a few miles south of Carlisle on the Midland Railway's magnificent Settle-Carlisle route, lost the use of its station from November 5 1956, but it remains virtually intact structurally. The MR wooden signalbox and the semaphores have gone, together with the goods yard and the neat paling fencing on the up platform, while on the down platform a modern chain link fence has been strung alongside the station building, which is now in private ownership. Above: On a gloriously sunny afternoon on April 6 1957, Horwich 'Crab' No. 42798 forges past with a Durranhill-Stourton goods.
Right: Class 25 'Rats' Nos. 25 324 and 25 276 double-head the diverted 3.37 am Stranraer Harbour-Euston parcels (3M07) through Cumwhinton on May 4 1985. *Robert Leslie/JB.*

LOW HOUSE CROSSING, which takes its name from a neighbouring farm, lies on the 'S&C' in the Eden Valley, just north of Armathwaite. Left: 'Royal Scot' 4-6-0 No. 46112 *Sherwood Forester* sprints over the crossing, watched by the signalman, with the down 'Thames-Clyde Express'. A single LMS vehicle in the middle of the train is accompanied by maroon Mk. 1 BR vehicles, most of which carry destination boards. Below: The same scene on May 4 1985 as Class 31s Nos. 31 438 and 31 467 work north with a Leeds-Carlisle train. The MR signalbox is still at work, although the traditional wooden gates have been replaced by full barriers with skirts, and flashing lights. *Robert Leslie/JB.*

Left: Looking towards Carlisle on August 8 1959 as the 4.37 pm Carlisle-Bradford stopping train, complete with a pair of six-wheeled milk tank wagons bringing up the rear, passes Low House behind Stanier '5MT' No. 44668. *Robert Leslie.*

Above: 'Royal Scot' 4-6-0 No. 46103 *Royal Scots Fusilier*, of Leeds Holbeck shed (55A), speeds into Armathwaite with an evening Glasgow-Leeds express comprised of very mixed stock. Armathwaite closed to goods from April 6 1964, after which the goods yard sidings were lifted: passenger services were withdrawn from May 4 1970. Right: No. 47 535 *University of Leicester* passes Armathwaite with the 10.47 am Glasgow-Penzance of May 4 1985. At this time the signalbox, although closed, survived along with the station building, now privately owned, and the goods shed. Below right: The 7 pm Carlisle-Appleby local leaves Armathwaite in the charge of Stanier 2-6-4T No. 42542. *Robert Leslie/JB*.

LANGWATHBY was another typical 'S&C' line station dating from the opening of the MR's new Anglo-Scottish route in 1876. It had its own buildings, signal box and goods shed, serving the local community until July 6 1964, when goods facilities were withdrawn, and for passengers until May 4 1970, when the station closed. Above: Fowler 4F 0-6-0 No. 43896 draws wagons of gypsum from Langwathby's sidings on November 3 1956. Note the cattle pens. Left: The same view in September 1984. The goods yard and shed is now owned by a haulage contractor, while the permanent way gang appear to have abandoned their chippings bin. *Robert Leslie/JB.*

KIRKBY STEPHEN WEST station was provided with up and down loops, a cattle dock, goods shed and coal yard. Goods facilities were withdrawn from September 28 1964 and the shed is now owned by a haulage contractor, but the loops and dock siding survived in 1985. Kirkby Stephen also has the very rare distinction of having been provided with a brand new signalbox in 1974: the MR box was demolished because of water in the foundations. Above: Riddles 9F 2-10-0 No. 92021 passes Kirkby Stephen with a southbound train of ingots while (right) a DMU runs past the same spot on September 5 1985. The station closed to passengers from May 4 1970. The cattle dock in 1985 was used for stabling engineers wagons — in the 1880s it handled around 300 wagons of livestock a year. *Ivo Peters/NH.*

AIS GILL SUMMIT, 1,169 ft above sea level and on the Cumbria county boundary today, was the end of the 'Long Drag' from Carlisle or Settle, and many a weary fireman must have been very glad indeed to pass the lonely signalbox and its loops, which are now memories. On September 5 1985 47 626 *Atlas*, passes with the 10.40 am Carlisle-Leeds (1E20). Below: In happier times, '9F' No. 92110 grapples with the 9.40 am Long Meg-Widnes anhydrite train of April 20 1967. The box has been rebuilt at the Midland Railway Centre, Butterley. *Ivo Peters/NH.*

ALSTON

THE little station at Alston, terminus of the 13¼-mile NER branch line from Haltwhistle, on the Newcastle-Carlisle route, lies just inside the Cumbria county boundary, although the greatest part of the brach itself is in neighbouring Northumberland. Opened in 1852, the line carried much coal mined near Lambley, and lead, mined around Alston. Economies started in 1955, when intermediate stations were reduced to unstaffed status, and the line was a prime target for Dr Beeching's infamous axe. However poor roads in the area helped local railway supporters with their case that closure would cause extreme hardship to the communities served by the railway. Even so, this only postponed what many saw as inevitable and when local road improvements enabled a replacement bus operation to start the branch closed, on May 1 1976. Original aims by the South Tynedale Railway Preservation Society to acquire and operate the railway as a

standard gauge link failed and the trackbed was sold to Northumberland and Cumbria County Councils. The STRPS then adopted the plan of building a 2ft gauge tourist railway on the trackbed, leased from CCC, and Alston has been redeveloped as an extremely attractive railhead, following landscaping and the provision of a car park. Initially operating

a two-mile section by diesel traction, the STR eventually aims to start steam haulage of its air-braked trains. The Alston station approach is pictured (top) in standard gauge days, with Worsdell class G5 0-4-4T No. 67315 in attendance, and (above) in September 1985, as converted into the STR's 2 ft gauge line. *LPC (Ian Allan Ltd)/NH.*

RAILS TO THE SOLWAY

RAILWAYS arrived on the Solway coast when the canal from Carlisle to Port Carlisle (opened 1823) was closed (1853) and track laid in the drained bed: it opened to rail traffic in 1854. A railway linking England's east and west coasts was achieved, but Port Carlisle was only accessible for two hours on each tide, and attention was thus focussed on a new branch to a proposed new deepwater dock at Silloth, 12¾-miles from Carlisle. This link, opened in 1856 overshadowed Port Carlisle's railway such that steam traction was abandoned in favour of a horse-drawn 'dandy'! This operated from 1857 until 1914 when steam locomotives returned, but traffic continued to dwindle and the Drumburgh-Port Carlisle line closed on May 31 1932. Above: 'J39' 0-6-0 No. 64930 approaches Burgh by Sands on June 1 1958 with the 10.15 am Carlisle-Silloth train. Left: the same scene in August 1984, nearly 20 years after closure on September 6 1964. The shallow cutting and its beautifully maintained track has been filled in and topped by an equally carefully tended lawn.
Robert Leslie/JB.

THE Silloth branch was a classic case of ill-considered speculation: opened in 1856, the dock it was supposed to serve was not started until 1857 and the first ship didn't arrive until 1859! Traffic never met expectations and failing fortunes after 1945 led to closure under Dr Beeching on September 6 1964 amidst much opposition in Silloth, which is shown (top) on June 13 1964 as CR 4-2-2 No. 1 and GNSR 4-4-0 No. 49 *Gordon Highlander* prepare to leave with a RCTS special from Leeds. Right: the same scene on August 22 1985. The station building survives, in modified condition, but little else betrays the railway's former presence. *Peter W. Robinson/ NH.*

DALSTON, the first station from Carlisle on BR's West Cumbrian Coast line, lies on the route of the Maryport & Carlisle Railway: this line, constructed in sections from both ends, met between Wigton and Aspatria on February 10 1845. Left: The 4.35 pm Carlisle-Barrow DMU passes Dalston on April 26 1985 as a pair of class 25 diesels marshal tank wagons in the oil depot which now occupies the former goods yard. Below: a similar viewpoint on August 4 1954 as Fowler 4F 0-6-0 No. 44510 roars towards Barrow with an evening goods train from Carlisle. The semaphore signals had gone by 1985, by which time the station was operating as an unstaffed halt.
Robert Leslie/JB.

CARLISLE-BARROW

DERWENT JUNCTION lies on the West Cumbrian coast line just north of the River Derwent in Workington. When this region was at its industrial peak, Workington was the hub of an intensively operated network of railways, principally serving the area's coal and haematite mines, iron works, and the docks. Top: Fowler 4F 0-6-0 No. 44461 plods north at Derwent Junction with a northbound trip freight on May 7 1963. Branching off to the left under the last wagons of the train is the sharply-curved connection of the line to Cockermouth, Keswick and Penrith, which disappeared from the network in 1966. From 1927 to 1965 a portion of the 'Lakes Express', from Euston, had arrived at Workington over this spur, after dividing from the Windermere portion at Oxenholme. The simplified connection to the right survived in April 1985, serving the nearby docks. *Ron Herbert/JB.*

OWRAH, located on the once-extensive network of railways around Whitehaven and Workington, was opened to eight traffic in November 1862 (for goods) and February 1864 (for passengers) by the Whitehaven, Cleator & Egremont ailway. The main traffic on this network of railways was the locally mined iron ore, which travelled north to Vorkington and south to Barrow, over railways abounding in sharp curves and stiff gradients. Passenger services were withdrawn from Rowrah on April 13 1931, but the railway remained open for goods traffic for a further 47 years. bove: on May 6 1963 Ivatt 4MT 2-6-0 No. 43004 shunts at Rowrah with the 12.10 pm Rowrah-Low Moor goods (9T60). owrah's northern link to the Cockermouth-Workington line at Marron Junction closed on May 3 1954 when imestone from Rowrah Hall Quarry was diverted through Moor Row: the end of operations at this quarry in 1978 left e truncated Moor Row-Rowrah line without traffic or purpose and it was lifted in 1980. The later picture was taken 1 March 1985. *Ron Herbert/JB.*

THE RAILWAY at Cleator Moor was the original branch from Moor Row built by the WCER in 1854, opened to mineral traffic in January 1856 and to passengers in July 1857. It was the opening of this railway which really prompted the industrialisation of West Cumbria and the large scale exploitation of the region's substantial mineral deposits: until the railway came, all ore and pig-iron had to be transported to the docks at Whitehaven by horse-drawn cart. Cleator Moor station disappeared with the withdrawal of passenger traffic between Moor Row and Siddick Junction, Whitehaven on April 13 1931, the Cleator Moor-Distington section remaining in use as a diversionary route until July 1963: the railway disappeared completely from Cleator Moor with the closure of the Moor Row-Rowrah link in 1978. Above: No 43004 wheels the 12.10 pm Rowrah-Low Moor goods through Cleator Moor on May 6 1963. Below: a similar viewpoint in March 1985. *Ron Herbert/JB.*

THIS dismal scene at Moor Row (left) belies the fact that the WCER workshops were once located here. In 1985 only weeds and clumps of bushes occupy the site of the engine sheds and busy repair shops. Until 1954 much of the motive power for the local lines was based at Moor Row, which was the junction of lines to Whitehaven and Workington (via Distington and Rowrah) and Sellafield. Constructed to tap West Cumbria's rich mineral wealth, the railway's fortunes faded with those of the iron and steel making industries. Above: Ivatt 4MT 2-6-0 No. 43004 rolls through Moor Row station (closed January 7 1935) on May 6 1963 with the 12.10 pm Rowrah-Low Moor goods. Left: In March 1985 the rusting and redundant rails at Moor Row awaited lifting for scrap five years after closure of Cumbria's last surviving iron ore mine at Beckermet, in October 1980, thus ending all traffic through Moor Row from Mirehouse Junction, near Corkickle.
Ron Herbert/JB.

BELOW: Ivatt 4MT 2-6-0 No. 43006 heads the 4.50 pm Millom-Moor Row freight (6T69) at Egremont on May 6 1963. The WCER opened its line to Egremont in January 1856 (to goods) and July 1857 (to passengers). This Railway carried vast amounts of ore to the coast at Corkickle and Whitehaven, where southbound trains had to reverse to run to Barrow. Consequently, a five-mile link from Egremont to Sellafield was opened in August 1869, to give southbound trains direct access to Barrow. Passenger services were first withdrawn between Sellafield and Whitehaven on January 7 1935, but this link was reinstated after the war on May 6 1946, only to be withdrawn permanently from June 16 1947. The Beckermet Junction-Sellafield section closed on January 18 1970, the northern Egremont-Whitehaven line lingering until 1980. ing until 1980. Right: the trackbed at Egremont in March 1985, the preserve of wildlife, walkers — and the graffiti artist. *Ron Herbert/JB.*

RAVENGLASS, an ancient Roman settlement, is equip-
ed with a distinctive station with staggered platforms
nd standard FR buildings. It was the point at which the
Ravenglass & Eskdale Railway, originally built to a
auge of 3 ft to transport haematite from mines at Boot to
he coast, diverged and ran inland. Opened in 1875, the
R&ER was put into the doldrums by the failure of the
mines in 1882 and closed in April 1913. It was subse-
uently rebuilt to 15 in gauge by renowned model
ngneer W.J. Bassett Lowke, who acquired the line in
early 1915. Top: In LMS days, an LNWR 'King George V'
4-4-0 runs through Ravenglass with an up passenger
train, which includes three cattle wagons at the rear. The
standard gauge goods yard is still operational with the
15 in gauge tracks on the extreme right. Above: a similar
viewpoint on July 6 1985 as the 9.15 am Carlisle-Barrow
DMU passes the goods yard site, now a tidily kept car
park for the R&ER, which uses the two Pullman cars for
members accommodation. The FR goods shed is used as
a workshop. *J. Kay Collection/JB.*

This page illustrates three phases in the life of the Ravenglass & Eskdale Railway, from 3 ft gauge days in 1906 to its role today as one of Lakeland's popular tourist attractions as a 15 in gauge railway. *Above right:* Manning Wardle 0-6-0T *Devon* (works No. 545 of 1875) at Eskdale Green station with a Bank Holiday working in 1906, comprised of both passenger and freight stock, normal practice in this era. *Centre Right:* This internal combustion locomotive (No. 2), hauling a train of Heywood-style passenger stock at Eskdale Green in 1927, was powered by a Lanchester Model 38 engine. Built in 1927 as a 2-6-2, using parts of the 1881-built steam locomotive *Ella* (an 0-6-0T), No. 2 was extremely powerful, but the engine was obsolete and when it broke down in 1930 it was withdrawn and subsequently dismantled. *Below:* 2-8-2 *River Mite* (built 1966) awaits the rightaway from The Green (as the station has been renamed in recent years, to avoid confusion with Dalegarth terminus, which is actually in Eskdale!) on July 6 1985. *Above & centre right: Mary Fair Collection/ R&ER. Below: John Broughton.*

BOOTLE was one of the villages served by the 33¼-mile Whitehaven & Furness Junction Railway, which linked the FR at Broughton with Whitehaven. The WFJR was opened in stages from the north, reaching Bootle in July 1850 and Broughton by the year end. Top: Bootle station in the opening years of this century. Note the inside-keyed track, superseded from 1914 by outside-keyed permanent way. The station features 'standard' FR buildings on the up platform, with a wooden shelter on the down side. Above: a similar viewpoint in April 1985: the railway and its facilities have been modernised but the station looks much as it did in Victorian and Edwardian times. The point in the bottom left corner of the older picture fed the station's former goods yard. *J.W. Pinch Collection/JB.*

MILLOM, in the far south west of the county, was a small village known as Holborn Hill when the WFJR arrived in 1850. Originally this company had planned to cross the Duddon from here on a massive 1¼-mile viaduct, but the high cost of this scheme prompted the adoption of an alternative route inland, crossing the river at a narrower point, and adding eight miles to the Barrow-Whitehaven journey. Today, the railway route from Millom to Ulverston, via Barrow, covers 25 miles, compared with seven miles 'as the crow flies!' The name Millom was adopted following the construction of the ironworks, fed by the neighbouring Hodbarrow mines, in 1867, after which the town grew very quickly. The station, which also took the new town's name, is pictured (top) in th early years of this century, prior to the construction c the platform awning by the FR, which took over th WFJR. Note the ornate gas lamp standards on the ver clean cattle dock and wooden FR brakevan beneath th loading gauge. Above: a similar viewpoint at Millom i 1985, looking towards Barrow, in April 1985. Much o the railway land in Millom was derelict in 1985, th double track main line carrying only its DMU passenge trains and a sparse goods service: only a single sidin survived in the once extensive goods yard. The lattic footbridge is of FR pattern.

J.W. Pinch Collection/ JB.

A 1¾-MILE branch from Millom was constructed to serve the Hodbarrow mines (the richest in the world at this time), and this link was completed in 1867, the same year the town's ironworks was built. The short branch carried ore from the mines to the works and in its century of operation Hodbarrow produced 25 million tons of haematite. Closure of the mines in March 1968 was followed six months later by closure of the ironworks, beyond which the Hodbarrow branch was closed on August 12 1968. The entire iron mining and making area was subsequently flattened and is now given over largely to sheep grazing and there are few reminders of the once extensive industrial past. Top: On August 27 1961, Fowler 4F 0-6-0 No. 44347 visits the Hodbarrow branch with the SLS/MLS 'Furness Rail Tour'. Below: the same location in April 1985. *Ron Herbert/JB.*

FOXFIELD, originally a joint WFJR/FR station, opened on August 1 1858, its branch line to Coniston starting operations nearly a year later, on June 18 1859. The station was enlarged in 1879 when the island platform was widened from 13 ft 6 in to 29 ft and several new buildings provided. It is this enlarged station which exists in simplified form today. Above: Ivatt 2MT 2-6-2T No. 41217 stands at Foxfield with the 1.27 pm from Coniston on July 18 1957. The Coniston line lost its passenger service from October 6 1958, freight services being withdrawn with the complete closure of the branch in 1962. Right: The 9.33 am Millom-Barrow DMU coasts into Foxfield on March 2 1985. The wooden passenger shelter survives and the signalbox is still at work, though the removal in 1985 of the crossover north of the station and plans to replace the crossing gates with barriers place its future in some doubt. *John Porter/JB.*

THE level crossing immediately south of Foxfield has hardly changed at all in the 22 years separating these two photographs, though the down siding and crossover have disappeared. Left: the 9.30 am Carlisle-Barrow DMU approaches the crossing on February 16 1985, the wooden main gates, wicket side gates and cast-iron warning signs all unchanged. Below: On a sunny afternoon on June 18 1963, Stanier 5MT 4-6-0 No. 45340 drifts towards Barrow at Foxfield with steam roaring from its safety valves.
John Porter/ JB.

COPPER mining at Coniston prompted construction of its railway, though decline of this industry in the 1860s and 1870s encouraged the FR to turn increasingly to tourism. Coniston station, with its beautiful 'Swiss cottage' style architecture sat high above the town where (Above) on July 18 1957 Driver Slater and Fireman Beck, of Carnforth shed, stand before 'Jubilee' 4-6-0 No. 45678 *De Robeck*, ready to return to Blackpool with a Tuesdays & Thursdays only passenger service. This was a rare visit by a 'Jubilee' — No. 45678 had a leaking cylinder gland and had been replaced on its Glasgow train at Preston by the Blackpool 'Black 5' originally rostered to run to Coniston. (*John Porter*). Above right: a similar viewpoint in July 1984 — the station has been utterly erased and redeveloped for light industry. (*John Broughton*). Left: '4F' 0-6-0 No. 44347 at Coniston with the 'Furness Rail Tour', August 27 1961. (*Ron Herbert*). Below left: the same location on July 15 1984. (*JB*).

THIS IS very much a modern 'past and present' comparison at Park South Juncion, Barrow's northern link with the Cumbrian Coast main line. Originally a triangle at this point allowed northbound departures from Barrow to turn either north or east, but the eastbound leg was removed in 1908. In 1984 the Barrow-Park South line was singled and the semaphore signals replaced by colour lights. Above: Class 47 No. 47098 approaches Park South Junction with a train of empty bogie bolsters in September 1984. Left: With the ballast clearly showing that the 'up' line has only recently been lifted, the 12.08 pm Lancaster-Whitehaven DMU approaches the Junction on April 24 1985. *Both: John Broughton.*

BARROW, known in the 1860s as the 'English Chicago' because of its very rapid growth and lawless atmosphere, eventually developed a complex and intensively worked railway system geared initially to the iron-making industry and later to shipbuilding. Barrow Central (now plain Barrow in Furness) station, was opened in 1882 at the point where the main road out of Barrow (today's A590) crossed the 5¼-mile loop line from Salthouse Junction to Park South Junction (originally Thwaite Flat Junction) on the coastal main line. The distinctive timber-framed station (top) with its substantial overall roof, was destroyed in a German bombing raid in May 1941: the ornate glass pavilion on the left, which housed FR 0-4-0 *Coppernob* was also destroyed and the locomotive, withdrawn in 1899, was taken to Horwich works for safekeeping. It is displayed at the National Railway Museum today, still showing shrapnel damage from the air raid. In 1959 a new station was constructed (pictured above) and on Monday August 26 a Western Region special headed by 47 *Windsor Castle* prepares to leave platform No. 1. *Ken Norman Collection/Phil Cousins.*

ISLAND ROAD STATION — or Barrow Shipyard as it was better known — served unadvertised trains carrying workers to the Vickers shipyard. This station was built in 1899 and during the Second World War up to five trains of between 10 and 12 coaches called each morning and evening. Island Road closed on July 3 1967 when workmens trains from Millom and Grange were diverted to Central station. Above: '4F' 0-6-0 No. 44347 stands at the station on August 27 1961 with the SLS/MLS Furness Railtour. Left: In January 1985 a shallow cutting newly planted with small trees marked the position of this outpost. *Ron Herbert/JB.*

FURNESS ABBEY station, opened in 1847, was located adjacent to the ancient ruins of Furness Abbey itself: the poet Wordsworth, well-known for his opposition to construction of the Windermere branch was also opposed to what he saw as the desecration of this area of Furness by 'the iron road'. The large Hotel next to the station was linked to its up platform by a covered walkway: in its day it was a fashionable and popular venue amongst the gentry of the day. The FR built a house at Abbots Wood, overlooking the station, for General Manager James Ramsden, whose special saloon had its own siding at Furness Abbey, from where he travelled to his office each day. The Hotel was closed by the LMS in 1938, after which it was used as a military barracks. Much of the hotel was later demolished, though one wing remains in use as a restaurant. The station closed on September 25 1950, the staggered platforms and buildings subsequently being erased from the landscape. Above left: the station in FR days, inside-keyed track indicating a pre-World War I picture. Above right: In April 1985 only the sleeper crossing and decaying stonework above the former subway entrance betray the position of the station. *J.W. Pinch Collection/ JB.*

ULVERSTON was in many ways a showpiece station for the Furness Railway, with elaborate cast-iron and glass canopies and an impressive station building and clock tower. The station was unusual in that there was a platform on the down side and an island platform between the tracks: the aim was to make life easier for passengers changing trains. Above: the west end of Ulverston station, looking towards Barrow, the station sign proclaiming: 'Ulverston, Junction for Lakeside Windermere and for Conishead Priory'. The Conishead line, branching away from the FR main line at Plumpton Junction (opposite the Lakeside branch) closed to pas- sengers on January 1 1917. The shortened line remained in use to serve the ironworks (which closed in 1938) and subsequently the massive Glaxo works, which is still in operation. Note the superb gas lamp lanterns, the ornate 'squirrel' platform benches and the very tall bracketed signals in the middle distance. Above right: a similar viewpoint in April 1985. *J.W. Pinch Collection/JB.*

THE
LAKESIDE
BRANCH

THE LAKESIDE BRANCH diverged from the FR main line at Plumpton Junction, 1½-miles east of Ulverston. Opened in June 1869, the branch was a manifestation of the FR's determination to exploit tourism to its advantage as iron ore, its traditional traffic, started to dwindle. The branch, which was double-tracked to Greenodd and single line thereafter, also carried substantial amounts of coal (for the Lake steamers), salt-petre and sulphur (for the gunpowder works at Low Wood and Black Beck), and ore (for the Backbarrow ironworks), while outward traffic included pig-iron, gunpowder, pit props, 'blue' from the Dolly Blue factory at Backbarrow and many thousands of bobbins from the mill at Stott Park, near Lakeside. Closed to passenger traffic in 1965 and freight in 1967, the Haverthwaite-Plumpton section is now but a memory.   Top: Coasting the final feet to Plumpton Junction on July 13 1960 is Fairburn

2-6-4T No. 42175 with a local train bound for Ulverston. By this time the Plumpton-Greenodd section had been singled, a sand-drag having been installed. Above: the same latter-day view from the bridge parapet with the cutting partially filled in. *John Porter/JB.*

TOP: Fowler 2-6-4T No. 42351 drifts towards Greenodd, south of Haverthwaite station, with a local train for Ulverston in the mid-summer of 1960. The year-round passenger service on the Lakeside branch was withdrawn on September 26 1938, summer services continuing until 1941 when they were suspended for the duration of the war. Seasonal trains returned in 1946, together with local services from Ulverston, but Haverthwaite and Greenodd stations closed to passengers in the same year. All passenger traffic was withdrawn on September 6 1965. The Backbarrow ironworks caused the line to be kept open for freight as far as Haver-thwaite, but its closure in 1967 signalled the end for t■ branch, which closed on April 24 1967. T■ Haverthwaite-Plumpton Junction section survived un■ 1971, by which time the locomotives and stock of t■ Lakeside & Haverthwaite Railway had been moved i■ and it was lifted by contractors. Above: The same sce■ today, looking much as it must have done before the F■ built the branch in the 1860s. The embankment wa■ transported to Greenodd by the lorry-load and tippe■ into the Leven estuary to provide the formation for t■ realigned A590 road — part of which also utilises t■ railway trackbed. *Mike Esau/NH.*

THE once-spacious branch terminus at Lakeside is much smaller than in its heyday, but steam trains run by the L&HR still make the traditional connection with the Windermere steamers. Top: Stanier 'Jubilee' 4-6-0 No. 45633 *Aden* rolls into Lakeside's 745 ft platform No. 1 in the mid-summer of 1960 with what appears to be an excursion train. Left : L&HR Hunslet 'Austerity' 0-6-0ST *Cumbria* (works No. 3794 of 1953) prepares to couple up to its train of Mk. 1 stock, prior to its last run of the day to Haverthwaite, on September 5 1985. The 205 ft platform adjacent to the loop is not used by L&HR passenger trains and the once-extensive yard is now a car park. *Mike Esau/NH.*

GRANGE-OVER-SANDS is one of the most attractive railway locations surviving in everyday use to be found in South Cumbria. Opened on August 10 1857 by the Ulverstone & Lancaster Railway Company (the archaic spelling of Ulverston was adopted), the splendid station buildings (built 1870s) are maintained in good condition by BR. The Furness Railway actively developed Grange as a 'Lancastrian riviera', providing ornamental gardens and a promenade of which the railway is an integral part. The overall effect is very similar to that created on the famous sea wall at Dawlish and Teignmouth, in Devon. Top: In 1905, Furness 0-6-0 No. 116 passe< Grange with a pick-up goods train of very mixe< composition. Ordered in 1881, the class of six engine (Nos. 114–119) were built by Sharp Stewart, No. 11 surviving until 1925, when it was scrapped by the LM! Above: the view from the same footbridge over the track on April 25 1983 as Class 40 'Whistler' No. 40080 passe< with a southbound evening tanker train fro> Whitehaven. The goods yard, and even the class 40 ar now pieces of railway history, their day done. *Peter V Robinson Collection/NH.*

ELA VIADUCT, on the 5¼-mile single line spur linking ιe FR main line at Arnside, with the Lancaster & arlisle Railway at Hincaster Junction, was a 26-arch ructure of impressive proportions. Crossing the aduct (Above) on June 30 1961 are Stanier 'Jubilee' 6-0 No. 45583 *Assam* and '5MT' No. 45385 with a ellington (Salop)-Windermere School excursion. These ains ran to Lakeside where the children boarded a indermere steamer for a trip to Bowness. The train would then run empty stock to Windermere where the children would rejoin for the next leg of the trip. Below: Looking at the scene from the same viewpoint today, you could be forgiven for not knowing the railway had ever laid its hand on the landscape. The line was closed north of the quarry at Sandside on September 9 1963, following the demise of the South Durham-Barrow coke trains, the remainder of the picturesque link following it into oblivion on January 31 1971. *Derek Cross/NH.*

BIBLIOGRAPHY

IF you have enjoyed this book, you may enjoy reading about the railways of Cumbria in more detail from the following list of books, all of which have been used in caption research for this title.

A Regional History of the Railways of Great Britain Vol 14 The Lake Counties by David Joy (David & Charles Ltd)
Over Shap to Carlisle — The Lancaster & Carlisle Railway in the 20th Century by Harold Bowtell (Ian Allan Ltd)
North of Leeds by Peter E. Baughan (Roundhouse Books)
Forgotten Railways Vol 1 North East England by Ken Hoole (David & Charles Ltd)
The Furness Railway by R.W. Rush (The Oakwood Press)
The Coniston Railway (The Cumbrian Railway Association)
Ratty's 100 by Douglas Ferreira (The Ravenglass & Eskdale Railway Ltd)
The Lakeside & Haverthwaite Railway by Howard Quayle & S.C. Jenkins (Dalesman Books)
The South Tynedale Railway by Thomas M. Bell (Old Queens Head)
The Kendal & Windermere Railway by Julian Mellentin (Dalesman Books)
Solway Steam by Stephen White (Carel Press)
Passengers No More by Gerald Daniels & Les Dench (Ian Allan Ltd)
LMS Engine Sheds Vol 4 by Chris Hawkins & George Reeve (Wild Swan Publications)
Railways of Cumbria by Peter W. Robinson (Dalesman Books)
Reflections of the Furness Railway by C.R. Davey (Lakeland Heritage Books)

ACKNOWLEDGEMENTS

SILVER LINK PUBLISHING would like to record their thanks to the many people who have assisted in any way, however small, with the production of this book, the first of a series looking at the changing appearance of British Railways.

Special thanks are due first of all to the many railwaymen in a variety of grades who assisted either with information or with the production of the modern pictures. Their help was gratefully received and much appreciated. Thanks also to the many photographers who provided the older pictures published in these pages: a special tribute is due to the late Derek Cross who warmed to this project very quickly and who came up with a good selection of photographs and lots of ideas, all delivered with his characteristic style and wit!

Useful help has also come from E.H. Booth & Co Ltd, for helping with a modern picture of the Windermere supermarket (formerly part of the station!), Ron Herbert, Ken Norman and Barry Metcalfe for assistance with captions, and Peter Van Zeller, of the Ravenglass & Eskdale Railway for pictures and information.

We would also like to record our gratitude to railway historian and photographer Peter W Robinson, for checking the text and making many useful comments and suggestions. Finally, apologies and thanks to anyone we may have omitted to mention!